The quarterly journal of *21st Century Chinese Poetry* was founded with the intention of introducing modern Chinese poetry to readers worldwide.

Modern Chinese poetry was born from the broader intellectual movement that took place in China in the early part of the 20th century, known as the May-Fourth Movement (1917-1921); for the first time in history, vernacular Chinese was accepted as a legitimate poetic voice. Since then, nearly a century has passed by and this poetic experiment hasn't stopped evolving but only accelerated recently because of the easy exchange of styles and ideas over cyberspace. This is an eye-opening, exciting and even confounding experience for both the poets and the readers.

The editor-and-translator team of *21st Century Chinese Poetry* selects some of the best poems written in Chinese by today's poets from all geographical areas.

Pathsharers LLC
560 N St SW, N-812, Washington DC 20024
Copyright @ 2012 by Pathsharers LLC

All poems are translated by permission of authors
All application for any use of any poems or quotations from them should be made to
Pathsharers LLC
560 N St SW, N-812, Washington DC 20024
editor@modernchinesepoetry.com

ISBN 978-06156781-8-4
ISSN 2166-3688 (Print--Bilingual)
ISSN 2164-1870 (Online)

21st Century Chinese Poetry

No. 4

Edited and Translated
by
Meifu Wang, Michael Soper, and Steven Townsend

A Pathsharers Book

CONTENTS

A Glimpse of Puxing Grade School 看了一回蒲杏小学

    by Niu Qingguo 牛庆国   9

A Powerful Pen 如椽之笔

    by Niu Qingguo 牛庆国   13

The Old Donkey 毛驴老了

    by Niu Qingguo 牛庆国   15

A Train Comes through the Sorghum Field 火车开进高粱地

    by Zhang Fanxiu 张凡修   19

The Spectacles 被看见

    by Zhang Fanxiu 张凡修   21

Letter to My Son 与子书

    by Zhang Fanxiu 张凡修   23

The Wintry Mix 雨夹雪

    by Ren Xianqing 任先青   25

The Dreams of Siberian Cockleburs 苍耳之梦

    by Ren Xianqing 任先青   27

I See Myself in the Chrysanthemum 从菊上看见自己

    by Ren Xianqing 任先青   29

I Can't Dawdle on Like This　我不再这样耗下去
　　by Sha Ma　沙马　　　　　　　　　　　　31

At the Café of California Sunshine　在加州阳光咖啡馆里
　　by Sha Ma　沙马　　　　　　　　　　　　35

Aboard the Ship　上了船
　　by Sha Ma　沙马　　　　　　　　　　　　37

Seeing and Being Seen　无题
　　by Yan Meimei　颜梅玫　　　　　　　　　39

Conversation with a Stranger　其实我们从未相逢
　　by Yan Meimei　颜梅玫　　　　　　　　　41

Five Glasses　五只玻璃杯
　　by Yan Meimei　颜梅玫　　　　　　　　　43

Summer Days 1.　夏日两则
The Difficulty of Being Free of Thoughts　啥也不想真的是很难
　　by Yi Hu　亦乎　　　　　　　　　　　　45

Summer Days 2.　夏日两则
The Horror of Perpetual Sunshine　天天阳光好其实是一种恐怖
　　by Yi Hu　亦乎　　　　　　　　　　　　47

I Want to Lean toward You　我想向你倾斜
　　by Yi Hu　亦乎　　　　　　　　　　　　49

Golden Rice 稻子黄了

    by Yang Kang 杨康　　　　　　　　　　　51

Bliss 幸福

    by Yang Kang 杨康　　　　　　　　　　　53

I Don't Like Windy Days 我不喜欢有风的日子

    by Yang Kang 文 杨康　　　　　　　　　　55

Bird within the Range of an Arrow 惊弦之鸟

    by Meifu Wang 王美富　　　　　　　　　　59

Dirt Road 土路

    by Meifu Wang 王美富　　　　　　　　　　61

Yesterday 昨天

    by Meifu Wang 王美富　　　　　　　　　　63

Information about Contributors　　　　　　　　66

Contact Information　　　　　　　　　　　　　70

看了一回蒲杏小学

文 / 牛庆国

像一颗松动的牙齿
在豁口处朝里张望
破了的玻璃还用报纸糊着
如果那是一张省报
说不定上面会有我的名字
如果我的名字能为孩子们挡一缕风寒
我肯定就有资格被写进校史里了
然而蒲杏小学早把我忘了
就像蒲杏村把好多人忘了一样
我也只是偶尔在履历表上
写下这个名字
最早的一张表上我只写蒲杏小学
后来就加上城关公社蒲杏大队
再后来还加上定西地区会宁县
现在要加上甘肃省了
如果在前面再加上中国
蒲杏小学就显得更加小了
比九牛一毛还小
如果在蒲杏小学后面再写下我的名字
念出蒲杏小学时就要换一口气了

A Glimpse of Puxing Grade School
by Niu Qingguo

It stands there like a loose tooth
peeking through a mountain gap.
The broken glass has been patched up with a newspaper
and I wonder if it's the Capital City Newspaper,
and could my name be in it.

A name, good enough to shield the children from the
 elements,
certainly should be entered into the school chronicle,
but I am sure Puxing School has forgotten me,
like Puxing Village has forgotten many villagers.

Only now and then, I would write down the school name
 on my resume.
In the earlier days, filling out Puxing Grade School was
 sufficient,
later on I would add Puxing Production Brigade,
then Dingxi District, and Huining Township.
Now I always put down Gansu Province,
and, if I should need to add the name of China to it,
Puxing Grade School would read infinitesimal,
less than a hair dropping among a herd of cattle.

如果在蒲杏小学后面再写下我的名字
念出蒲杏小学时就要换一口气了
记得操场边上有我栽的白杨树
只是现在只剩一根白杨橡了
作为一根旗杆立在一年级教室门前
像一根大铅笔
在黄土里按住一个孩子们忘了的生字
这是2005年秋的一个星期天
我真想翻墙进去
看看我办过的黑板报还在不在

Now, add to Puxing Grade School my name,
and you won't be able to say the whole string in one
    breath.

The birch tree that I planted on the edge of the school field
has only the tree trunk left, used as the flag pole
in front of the first grade classroom.
It looks like a big pencil, anchoring on the yellow earth
some unforgettable vocabulary.

This is a Sunday in the autumn of 2005,
and I wish I could just climb over the fence
to see if the chalkboard bulletin
I edited for the school is still up.

如椽之笔

文 / 牛庆国

只有树　才是真正的
如椽大笔
即使风花雪月　树
也写的是大意境

大西北的大　就是
大风大雨　大起大落
也只有树的挥洒
才能写到悲壮的境地

悲壮　就悲壮个
飞沙走石　气壮山河
狂草的艺术
靠的就是这种气势

悲壮　也就悲壮个
北风呼啸　大雪纷飞
这飞白的笔力
可千万要遒劲

A Powerful Pen
by Niu Qingguo

Only a tree can be said to be a power pen.
In a blizzard, it's the trees that give the landscape
a sense of vastness.

The vastness of the northwest gives rise to
sweeping winds and rain, awesome and erratic,
and only the wild swaying of the trees
embues the place with the spirit of tragic heroism.

Tragic and heroic, you see it in the double image
of blowing sand and flying rocks, fluid and unconstrained,
the same spirit in the art of a wild cursive writing.

Tragic and heroic, you see it in the double image
of howling arctic winds and snow storms,
the same vigor as when a thick paint brush
flies across a sheet of paper.

毛驴老了

文 / 牛庆国

帮父亲耕了多年地的毛驴 老了
它的老 是从它前腿跪地
直到父亲从后面使足了劲
才把车子拉上坡的那天开始的
那天 父亲搂着毛驴的瘦腿
像搂着一个老朋友的胳膊
父亲说 老了 咱俩都老了
现在 它或许知道自己不中用了
水不好好喝 草也不好好吃
穿了一辈子的破皮袄
磨光了毛的地方 露出巴掌大的伤疤
我几次让父亲把它卖掉
但几次父亲都把它牵了回来
像早年被老人逼着离婚的两个年轻人
早上出去晚上又怯怯地回来了

The Old Donkey
by Niu Qingguo

It's old, the donkey who plowed our field year after year.
The first revelation came the day it knelt on its front legs
and the cart was pushed uphill,
by father, with every thread of his strength.

That evening, father embraced the donkey's skinny legs
like a man circling his arm around an old friend's shoulders.
He said, "We are old, you and me."

Now, the donkey seemed to know it served no purpose
and lost interest in water and hay.
The ragged coat that it had worn for a lifetime
showed a bald, palm-size scar.

I told father to take it to the market,
but they always came home together
like a young couple, forced by parents to divorce,
leaving home at dawn and timidly returning together at
    dusk.

那天我从屋里出来
它把干枯的脑袋搭在低矮的圈墙上
声音颤抖着 向我呼唤了几声
那么苍凉 忧伤
父亲说 他知道毛驴想说什么

The other day, I stepped outside
and saw the donkey, chin on the fence;
it beckoned me with a trembling voice,
so bleak and so sad,
but father said he knew what it meant to say.

火车开进高粱地
文 / 张凡修

交出铁轨
秸杆躺下来，让远方的亲人
从自己的身体上回家

无论走多远，走不出高粱地
左旱路，右水路
秋风一年一吹
铁轨一根一根站着，长高

交出行程
高粱地掏空秋天，掠过瞬间的苍老
穗子内心辽远，扎成一把一把笤帚
扫净了通往村外的冬雪

无数亲人，又坐在高粱地里
他们都成了
开走的火车

A Train Comes through the Sorghum Field
by Zhang Fanxiu

Hand over your iron tracks.
The sorghum stalks lay down
to allow folks from far away to return,
riding on their fallen bodies.

However far the journey is,
overland or over the water,
it never leaves the sorghum field.
And when the autumn wind blows,
those iron stalks stand up,
one by one, looking tall.

Turn in your itinerary.
The sorghum has consumed all of autumn,
aged in a blink of time,
but its grains are broad-minded,
soon to be bundled into brooms
to clear a snow-free trail out of the village.

So many of our folks returned home
to sit in the sorghum field,
and they have become
the train that has passed on.

被看见

文 / 张凡修

一种奇怪的声音在红松林与玉米林间
喧响。很多人朝纵深走去
去参加,一个护林人的白事儿

护林人便是归去了。
喧响源自一群吹鼓手手中的乐器
被看见
而喧响,去那儿的人,没心思听

他们只盯着红松林与玉米林
不可捉摸地,发呆。

白事儿的午餐很单调
松仁玉米和大锅炖菜
被看见。
所有人手中的筷子
被看见——

一齐伸向松仁玉米。
那静悄的悲伤,挟起,两座森林
——被看见。又空旷得
什么也没有。

The Spectacles
by Zhang Fanxiu

Some hubbub is going on
in the redwood forest by the cornfield.
People file into the woods
for the forester's funeral.

So the forester has passed on.
The din and the tumult are from the band,
which is seen rather than heard,
because people there are in no mood for music.

They stare at the redwoods and the cornfield.
Their minds meander, seemingly aimless.

A simple meal is served at the funeral—
corn and stewed vegetables,
a spectacle by itself.
So many chopsticks are held in the hands,
a spectacle too, as they come down together
at the pine seeds and corn kernels.

The unspoken sadness, the chopsticks, and forests
are true spectacles, but the field is so empty,
and so removed.

与子书

文 / 张凡修

我什么都可以交出。唯独
这所老房子,不能给你
——就在这儿养老啦
这是当年你母亲我俩
脱了六天泥坯,偷大队十五棵柳树
自家稻草,自家高粱秫秸,自家高粱米饭
请四人帮工建起来的:
九米六长,五米六宽,两米八高
前后檐三七,俩房山四八
冬暖。夏凉。
孙子就搁这儿,我们抚养
上学你母亲送,放学我负责接
这房子与泥土相连,地气重
孩子不爱闹毛病。
我们腿脚都利索,但不愿踏进你的楼房
实在不忍心那个布袋套在鞋子上
去一趟,连印痕
都不曾留下

Letter to My Son
by Zhang Fanxiu

I am willing to give you everything that's mine.
But not this old house, which you must do without
----this is where I want to grow old----
It's your mom's and my efforts combined,
drying wet bricks for six days,
stealing 15 willow trees from our production brigade,
cutting rice and sorghum stalks from our own field,
and cooking rice and sorghum for our four helpers.
9.7 meters long, 5.6 meters wide,
and a standing room of 2.8 meters,
the front and the back walls are 21-centimeter thick,
and the longitudinal ones are 32 centimeters thick,
just right for winter and summer.

Leave our grandson here, we will bring him up;
the morning trip is for your mom, but I'll pick him up after
    school.
This house sits right on the earth, whose breaths
will keep the ailments from children.
Our legs are quick, but they do not fancy your high-rise
    apartment.
What a funny feeling to slip the plastic covers over our
    shoes!
We were there, but not a single footprint
was left behind.

雨夹雪

文 / 任先青

我说的是阴云 会写字
写又湿又冷的 雨夹雪

风是不会敛声息气的
狠狠摇动树 不让鸟们站稳
鸟便把自己掷向远处
带着世袭的嘴唇

雨渐渐雪了 地渐渐白了
这天气 我等待的人来不了了

炉火很旺
一壶诗汩汩作响
我用叹息 倒出体内灰烬
忽然间很想花光这满地银子
租一个唐朝的我回来 与之对饮
做一回自己的领袖 醉！

The Wintry Mix
by Ren Xianqing

Dark clouds, it looks to me they also know how to write,
scribbling out words damp and cold, a wintry mix.

You bet the wind won't hold back;
it shakes the trees so relentlessly that the birds lose their
    perches,
and decide to go into exile,
taking with them their playbill.

The rain is now turning into snow, covering the ground
    with white;
in such weather, my friend won't be able to keep his
    appointment.

But the fire is burning hotter than before
and the pot of poetry is about to boil.
With a sigh, I decant all the ashes in me,
and feel the urge to squander away all I have
to meet an older edition of me,
from the Tang Dynasty, to drink together,
and to command life as I please.
Get drunk!

苍耳之梦

文 / 任先青

路边　崖旁　散淡生长
用崭新或陈旧的绿
分叉　簇拥日子的八个方向
不求有声　但求有色　只求秋来
结出多刺的种子　心情随风
勾住我的小小忧伤

不知苍耳是否有梦
不知是否梦到过天堂
抱着入药、入世的爱与想法
民歌一样可信　然后宁静地归隐
把一年卑微的梦　慢慢闭上……

The Dreams of Siberian Cockleburs
by Ren Xianqing

On the edge of the road or on the cliff, they perch
    precariously;
some in brilliant green, others in dull green,
but each compact life opens up into eight forks.

They're content to remain silent, but live for colors,
waiting for the fall to bear thorny seeds which just float in
    the wind.
They happen to know how to hook away my tiny sorrows,
    too.

I wonder if the cockleburs dream like we do.
Have they ever dreamt about heaven?
How do they grasp the idea of being medicinal herbs,
participants in the world?

Today they are as true as folk songs, but will withdraw
    silently,
slowly shutting down a year's worth of dreams . . .

从菊上看见自己

文 / 任先青

古朴的城墙下
一朵菊 寂寞地开放
很像秋天忍住的最后一句话
又像浪迹多年的孩子 深夜返家
在我肺腑上
旋转一把疼痛的钥匙

从菊上 我看见了自己
满头白色花瓣 被季节忽略
一些叹息已随风飘走
最怅惘 这些年我与你天各一方
手执宗教相互翘望
幸有遗爱 供我一点一点忧伤

I See Myself in the Chrysanthemum
by Ren Xianqing

Below the antiquated city wall,
a Chrysanthemum is still open, all by itself,
as if autumn has left us with an unspoken word.

It looks like a tired child, returning at night after years of roaming.
I feel someone is turning a key in my heart,
and it hurts.

And I see myself in the chrysanthemum,
in its white petals and the neglected look.
So many sighs are gone with the wind,
but a sorrow lingers because you live a world apart;
a long glance can't bridge the difference of our beliefs.
But I feel traces of your love, and that is my consolation.

我不再这样耗下去

文 / 沙马

这几天我一直咳嗽。
我不去想皮诺曹是怎样从木偶人变成孩子。
不去解释瘸腿猫为何要骗瞎眼狐狸。
也懒得陪儿子玩假面龙，废品战士
邪神消灭者和R—CKMB泡沫人游戏。

我一声接一声咳，对生活失去耐心。
但垃圾得及时处理。
精神有问题得及时处理。
我打开电视我看见把头发卷成波浪型的
播音员讲反恐主义，种族歧视
肉体炸弹和海湾战争，讲洗面奶
甘油，鱼子酱，脑百金和一台D—5912牌榨油机。

我咳得不行了
我不再把"河豚"说成"鱼"
不再用幻想来保存躯体。

I Can't Dawdle on Like This
by Sha Ma

Too much coughing these days.
I can't afford to question how Pinocchio turned into a
    human child
or the crippled cat tricked the blind fox.
I can't just fool around with my son on video games like
Masked Dragon, Junk Warrior, the Wicked Eraser, or R-
    CKMB.

The coughing won't stop, and my patience with life is gone,
but the garbage can't wait,
and I must deal with mental stress as it comes.
But the TV commentator with a wavy coiffure
is talking nonstop about anti-terrorism, racial
    discrimination,
body bombs, the gulf war, face cream,
glycerin, caviar, melatonin and even a vegetable-oil press.

This cough is killing me.
I should stop calling the river dolphin a fish,
or relying on fantasies to sustain me.

不再相信"明天我会考虑一切。"这句话。
不认为从 B 中减出的某物
加到 A 上就能得到平衡
不再把"灵魂"理解为"幽灵"。
不。不。再这样耗下去
我只得和这个世界说声，拜拜。

I shouldn't trust the sentence "I will think through it
    tomorrow"
or assume harmony will come from redistribution.
And, stop thinking souls are just ghosts.
No. No. If I don't stop dawdling like this,
I will have to wave to the world and say: bye-bye.

在加州阳光咖啡馆里

文 / 沙马

你是女幻想家,坐在加州阳光咖啡馆里
和我谈鸟儿,水獭,长颈鹿
和非洲的斑马
它们的生活性习和来自不同的区域
像赵忠祥叙说的《人与自然》
以此来满足我的好奇心。
这是没用的,我是一个矮小的人
在童话里长大
看见过白雪公主,镜子和苹果。
我的器官有了警觉
在表面上装出一副无所谓的样子
尽量不拿眼睛看你。
人与动物的区别是精神现象上的问题
女幻想家也有身体
需要用不同的方式周旋。
我厌倦了咖啡里
一种夜晚的形式感。
我是个中年人,机会来了就下手
不在现象上饶舌,不排除
在这个咖啡馆里掀开裙子看看你

At the Café of California Sunshine
by Sha Ma

You are a romantic lady, sitting in California Sunshine
and talking with me about birds, otters, giraffes,
African zebra,
their behaviors, and native habitats;
it reminds me of Mr. Zhao's TV show "Man and Nature".

You do it to satisfy my curiosity about you.
But really, it's quite hopeless, I am a dwarf,
having lived through the fairy tales like a child
with Snow White, the mirror and the apple.
Right now my body is sending out warning signals,
but I cover them up with nonchalance
by taking my eyes away from you.

We are different from other animals in mental framework.
This romantic lady has a body and flesh, too,
but I must go about it in another way.

I am sick of the fabricated night ambiance in the cafe.
I am now middle-aged, an opportunist,
and I won't succumb to ambiance,
waste my breaths on words, or preclude
the chance of looking under your skirt in the cafe.

上了船

文 / 沙马

上了船就别说些
令人沮丧的话
别议论资本主义国家里
发生的那些鸟事。

一屁股坐在轮船的铁板上
是不是有些麻木。

要向站在窗口的
小女孩学习
她一边吃着豆子
一边望着海水

Aboard the Ship
by Sha Ma

Now we are on board, let's not
bring up any depressing topics;
no more debates about the pet peeves
in those capitalist countries.

Sit your ass down on the metal board.
Doesn't it make you feel a little numb?

We've got to learn to be
that girl by the window,
eating dry beans
and looking out at the sea.

无题

文 / 颜梅玖（玉上烟）

雷平阳说，罗公远的隐身术
到宋朝就失传了
事实证明，在我们美丽的国度
很多人都精通这种法术，但我们不像罗公远
动辄掰着指头数落皇帝，吓坏他
也不像一叶障目那个傻瓜
有人很干脆，不与虎谋皮
但坚持目盲
有人住庙宇，上佛堂，悠悠然吟诵晓风明月
暗通上下山的路径
有人懂得什么时候要管住自己的嘴巴
在生活附近生活的隐形人
几十年也没长出什么坏脾气
不左看，不右看
就是路边那颗被碾碎的头颅，也看都不看

Seeing and Being Seen
by Yan Meimei

The kungfu of being invisible was lost
before the Song Dynasty, a modern scholar claimed.
The truth is that in our beautiful country
there are still many who practice this art superbly,
but they differ from the old master,
who used it when chiding the emperor, to frighten him.
Neither do our experts delude themselves like some ancient
    fool;
they do not fault the idea of not seeing
but know crisply clear not to ask a tiger for its hide.
Some live in the monasteries in order to pray at the alter
and chant surreal verses about nature's beauty.
They know every secret path in and out of the mountains
and when to hold their tongues.
They live invisibly at life's outskirts
with a perfect temperament year after year,
and, without looking right or left,
the crushed skull by the road is now invisible to them.

其实我们从未相逢
文 / 颜梅玖（玉上烟）

你几次欲言又止，这并不妨碍我
看到事物的本身。虽然股票，天气，以及我的新疾
最近都出现了晦暗不明的迹象
有人焦虑，有人发疯，有人无动于衷
就像那瓶被我弄洒的法国香水
空瓶子此刻是一个极好的隐喻。它不仅仅提示我
要对生活倍加小心。昨天喝酒时
有的人谈起正史和野史，口若悬河
但我们都知道哪个更真实。就像香水散后
生活无疑更可靠一些。瞧
香气退后，忧伤络绎不绝地来了
泪水络绎不绝地来了
有人开始忏悔，有人开始否定，也有不谙世事的人
继续热爱和惶恐……

Conversation with a Stranger
by Yan Meimei

You moved your lips, but held back the words,
but that didn't stop me from seeing the naked truth.
Even though the stock prices, weather, and my latest illness
all seem to move in dubious directions these days,
causing some to be depressed or hysterical,
there are a few who remain unmoved,
just like the reactions to a tipped bottle of French perfume.
But now I think the empty bottle is a perfect metaphor for
    life:
Take heed of living!

Yesterday, over a bottle of wine,
a friend brought up an historic event,
both its official and folksy versions,
but we all knew which version to choose,
not unlike preferring the unscented part of the day
after the perfume wears out.
That's when sorrows overflow
and tears fall.
Some will repent or learn to withdraw,
but a few others, unfamiliar with the world,
will continue to love and live fearfully...

五只玻璃杯

文 / 颜梅玫（玉上烟）

第二只清洗时失手打碎。第一只
来不及上手，毁于滚烫的开水
第三只，正在掉落的
途中。余下的两只
我预感它们迟早落地。这些年
我早已适应了碎裂之声，甚至喜欢
刹那间的快意。无非是失去了一些杂念
了结了因缘。人到中年
不过就是把一个个杯子默默地
反复擦洗

Five Glasses
by Yan Meimei

The second glass slipped from my hand while I was
    washing it.
The first one was not even in my hand when it cracked
in boiling water. The third one is now taking its fall.
There are two left,
and I foresee their fall too.
Years ago I began to get used to the sound of breaking,
and even enjoying an instant of exhilaration, which must
    have to do
with breaking away, from wants and entanglements.
My life has reached its midpoint, and I oddly feel
I am that glass that's being washed
again and again.

夏日两则,1
啥也不想真的是很难
文 / 亦乎

今天阳光真好
真的是蛮好蛮好
真想脱个一丝不挂
找个避风的地方
有树林的山坡,或者
垂着紫藤的墙角
就那么躺着
啥也不想

其实啥也不想
真的是很难
亦乎摆脱不了的
放不下的是写小说
一个关于谋杀的
文艺小说

小说的开头一句
是这样
　"xx 被谋杀的那天早上
还没来得及吃早餐
通常,他的早餐是一碗
热干面,有时加一份煎蛋

Summer Days, 1
The Difficulty of Being Free of Thoughts
by Yi Hu

Today's sunshine, how beautiful it is!
It is really, really nice indeed
that I wish to slip off my clothes
and be somewhere sheltered from the wind,
perhaps a slope in the woods, or
a corner under the vine wall,
just to lie down
and be free of all thoughts!

But it's easier said than done
to be free of thoughts.
Something is keeping me from being liberated--
a novel I feel I must write
that has a murder plot in it--
a romance novel for bedside reading.

The first lines should begin
like this:
" The morning when xx was murdered,
he hadn't had breakfast yet,
which, as a habit, consisted of
hot noodle soup, and a serving of fried eggs...

夏日两则，2
天天阳光好其实是一种恐怖
文 / 亦乎

今天的阳光比昨天还好
那其实是一件可怕的事
昨天，阳光好亦乎一丝不挂
想着写关于谋杀的文艺小说
今天，阳光好亦乎就有一种
恐怖感，是真的
如果再这么好下去
没有雨，也没有让人头发
微微飘起的风
那，那"真是不文艺"
亦乎肯定是
"不能安下心来"
写花花想看的，特
悬疑的，又是那特什么的
关于谋杀的小说

如果每个人都不能
安下心来
干自己想干的事
那只能说明
"今天的阳光"真的
真的是太厉害了

Summer Days, 2
The Horror of Perpetual Sunshine
by Yi Hu

Today's sunshine is prettier than yesterday's,
but there is something horrific about it.
Yesterday, I lay down in the sun nude
pondering how to compose a murder story,
so horrific that the sunlight seems simmered
in a different atmosphere today. It is too bad
if things continue in this direction
without a drop of rain or a wisp of wind
to stir my hair.

In that case, the romance will be lost,
and most definitely
I will lose my cool and be unable to write--
the heightened suspense
and other extraordinary features,
just what a thriller needs.

If every single person is like me,
feeling too ill-at-ease
to pursue what he wants,
it only tells the fact that
today's sunshine, really,
has gone overboard.

我想向你倾斜

文 / 亦乎

我想向你倾斜
最温柔地向你倾斜
我想触摸你的敏感
你心中最敏感的紫色

我想,最温柔地想
想那倾斜一刻
你心中最敏感的紫色
是否能涂抹我的额头

I Want to Lean toward You
by Yi Hu

I want to lean toward you;
doing it so tenderly,
to feel your sensitive heart,
that purple heart of yours.

Most tenderly I ponder
the moment when I lean toward you:
Will you smear purple on my forehead
and anoint me to be your friend?

稻子黄了

文 / 杨康

风一吹,蚂蚱就跳到
正在扬花吐穗的稻子上
紧接着稻子就黄了。先是几株
是一片片黄的稻子,再就是
山沟沟里被感染着的稻子
所有的稻子羞涩起来,低着头
稻子黄了。乡村热闹起来
那些汉子们,和看家
的媳妇们都没得清闲
就连躲在树上的麻雀
也叽叽喳喳。老黄牛们还能
在田间地头啃点青草
娃娃们追着跑着,尾随大人
暮色暗下来,娃娃们还没尽兴呢
可是稻子黄了。娃娃们盘算着
稻子一黄,再过几天就要开学了

Golden Rice
by Yang Kang

The wind blows, sending the crickets up the rice stalks,
inflorescent and maturing; in no time,
the rice will be golden. Starting with a few stems,
then a few paddies, then, almost infectiously,
every single stalk in the valley will look shy,
bending its head.

The rice is golden.
The countryside turns boisterous.
Those macho guys, and women who ordinarily
only keep houses abandon their pastimes.
Even the sparrows that hide in the trees are chatty.
Yellow cattle still graze here and there between crops;
children chase and run, tagging along after grownups,
still in a playful mood, even when dusk descends.

But the rice is now golden.
The children count on their fingers.
When the rice is golden, school will start
in just a few days.

幸福

文 / 杨康

在腊月里，谈到棺材
谈到奶奶身体虚弱。这些话
是父辈们在晚饭后围着炉火说的
火焰不断上窜，这么多幸福和温暖
山坡阳面，万物之上阳光普照
野山药在荆棘丛中动了动身
泥土解冻。田地都开始复苏
再过些天，再暖和点，阳光再
稠密些，就得下种了，多么幸福
我们在泥土里种下玉米和土豆
按时拔草、施肥，闲下来会看见
绿苗向上。风，翻过山头
风在田野里大张旗鼓地奔跑起来

Bliss
by Yang Kang

In December, a coffin was mentioned,
as well as Grandma's frailty. These words
were uttered by my father and uncles
after dinner around the stove;
the flames rose up one by one.
What bliss and warmth!

On the sunny slope, all is bathing in the sun.
The mountain yams swell under the thorn bush,
and the earth is thawing. The field awakens too,
and in a few days when it warms up more,
when the sunrays get denser,
it will be time for sowing. What bliss!

We will bury the seeds of corn and potatoes,
then weed, feed, and watch, when not busy,
green sprouts emerging. The wind will
climb over the hills, and the exuberant wind
will run across the field.

我不喜欢有风的日子

文 / 杨康

我不喜欢有风的日子,我怕
一阵从南到北的风,腰肢一扭
就把我单薄的父亲,刮到脚手架边

只要起风,多数的时候就会有雨
更多的时候,父亲就会无处可归
风吹散了父亲刚刚倒出来的水泥
风又把水泥吹到老板身上,吹到父亲眼里
这可恶的风,就这样白白吹走
父亲的半斤汗水。风,吹来暮色和寒意
风吹着,父亲就开始想家,想远方的儿子
时间比陷入泥淖还要缓慢
没有电视和空调,甚至没有一张
舒适的床,用来安放父亲疲惫的心

I Don't Like Windy Days
by Yang Kang

I don't like windy days. I fear
a southerly wind, with a shear,
would blast my skinny father
right to the edge of the scaffold.

When the wind is blowing,
it's often raining too,
and most of the time
Father would have nowhere to hide.
The wind blows, scattering the cement Father just poured,
spraying it into his eyes and on his boss.
This damn wind, it blows and wastes
a half pound of father's sweat.
Dusk and chill come with it.
In the wind, Father begins to feel homesick
missing his sons, and time passes slower
than if it is trapped in the mud.
There is no TV, no air conditioning,
no comfortable bed to rest his tired heart.

他想着他的儿子,一个在延安,一个在重庆
在广播里听到与这两个城市有关的讯息
他都会忐忑不安,彻夜无眠,直到风止

我不喜欢有风的日子,风是父亲的苦难
我怕什么时候风一吹,就把我的父亲
从这个世界,吹到另一个世界

He misses his sons, one in Yan'an, one in Chongqing;
and if the radio happens to broadcast
news from either city, he gets worried,
hardly sleeping till the wind dies.

I don't like windy days.
Wind is a hardship for Father.
I'm so worried an unpredictable wind will blow,
taking with it my father
from this world to another.

惊弦之鸟

文 / 王美富

我画不出你的红。
你
用左翼和右翼
迎接一束彩虹,
以五花八门的颜色
刺痛我的眼瞳;
像温柔的刀锋,
像美丽的刀锋;
但无论怎么痛,
我情愿死于你的剑下,
愚蠢地等待重生,
如凤凰从灰烬里飞升。

我无法模仿你的歌声。
时而幽婉,时而英勇,
只有庙宇的暮鼓晨钟
还有天堂的灵魂
与你神会心融,
而我
只能是若即若离,
仿如胸怀大志的败兵,
唯恐一个小小的举动
就让你受惊;
我不自觉地袒护你,
难道你就住在我心中?

Bird within the Range of an Arrow
by Meifu Wang

I can hardly paint your color of red.
You
open up your right wing and left wing
to intercept the rainbow,
reflecting the spectrum of colors
that pierce my eyes;
they are like tender arrows,
beautiful arrows,
but I don't mind that they hurt;
I'd rather die with these arrows
and, without questioning, wait for a resurrection,
like a phoenix from the ashes.

I know not how to mimic your singing,
sometimes melancholic, sometimes heroic;
only the bells or drums from the temple
and those souls in heaven
know how to synchronize with your spirit,
as for me
I only watch you from a distance,
almost like an ambitious soldier, now defeated,
taking care of every small movement
lest it would scare you into flight.
For some unknown reason, I wanted to protect you.
Is it true that you live in my heart?

土路

文 / 王美富

我和脚前的土路有点相似,
没什么现代元素,使不出多少力气,
面对照相机,总会蒙上一圈黄晕;
如果想去欣赏那心爱的,婆娑的椰林,
还得徒步一个早晨又一个下午,
可是它总是散发出迷人的芳馥。
每当我闭上眼睛,就听见脚步——
三五成群,轻快,灵活,脚步的合唱,
就像乘载歌声的翅膀——于是我不再绝望,
也许那时正是早晨,或是黄昏。

Dirt Road
by Meifu Wang

The dirt road and I, we resemble each other—
very few modern elements, not very durable.
In a camera lens, you will see us through a yellow haze.
If you wish to follow this road to the lovely coconut beach,
it would take you a morning or an afternoon on foot,
but there is always a charming fragrance along the way.
When I close my eyes, I hear footsteps—
in groups of threes and fives, light and lively,
a chorus of footsteps, like a song with wings
rising, so I am no longer in despair.
I will listen to it in the morning.
I will listen to it in the afternoon.

昨天

文 / 王美富

昨天已经来过,
证据就在我的衣襟上——
嬉闹中留下的淡淡酒痕,
木桌上沉淀的花香。

虽然我没有殷勤款待,
曾经独守阳台,
被牵牛花的靛蓝弄得心痒;
那时他悄悄打身边溜过,
去他得去的地方。

看,我为他敞开的窗帘还开着,
月光胆大地进到房里…

有时我沉湎于昨天的昨天,
(何时开始养成的习惯?)
耳边传来熟悉的琴韵和诗歌;
如果野雁正巧飞过,羽毛夹带云彩的光泽,
我就松一口气:确实
天地的聪慧足以弥补我的缺失。

也就在昨天,猎人的枪声响彻云霄,

Yesterday
by Meifu Wang

Yesterday has been here,
the evidence can be seen on my collar—
wine stains from laughter and play
and the flower scents that seeped into the table.

I wasn't always attentive,
alone on the garden porch sometimes,
dazzled by the blue morning glories;
it was then when he passed me by
to meet his next appointment.

Can you see? The curtains are still open from his last visit;
the moonshine enters the room so boldly…

Sometime I am lost in yesterday and its yesterdays,
(Since who-knows-when this has become a habit?)
hearing old songs and poems,
and, if the flamboyant cranes happen to fly by,
I would sigh: indeed
the universe can't be tarnished by a small blemish such as
    me.

It was yesterday, too, when a gunshot broke the silence of
    the sky;

宝贵的生命从高空回旋坠落，
全身被黑夜笼罩，
明天不再周而复始。

越来越深，越来越多的迷惑
如昨天的背影重重；
我终于开口：
为什么他来了又走了，
把有的人牵引，却依然把我留下？
然而我只有倾慕，没有懊悔，
只要能够再一次看见太阳。

a precious life spiraled down from high above.
His body enveloped by darkness;
there wouldn't be another tomorrow for him.

More and more, deeper and deeper doubts
stood like yesterdays' overlapping shadows.
Finally, I asked
why he came and went,
taking along a few of us, but leaving me behind?
But I will have only adoration and no regrets
as long as I see the sun rising, before my eyes.

Information about Contributors

The Editor-and-Translator Team:

Meifu Wang: Ms. Wang is the chief editor and translator of this issue of *21st Century Chinese Poetry*. Born and grew up in Taiwan, Meifu Wang earned her BA in Foreign Languages and Literature from National Taiwan University. Her poetry can be seen in various Chinese literary journals. She lives in Washington DC.

Michael Truman Soper: Mr. Soper recently joined the editor-and-translator team of 21st *Century Chinese Poetry.* He assisted with the translation and revision of all poems in this issue. Born in Washington, DC, in 1946, he began writing poetry in high school, and studied creative writing, briefly, at UVA. He was a submarine sailor during the Vietnam War, after that, a newspaper typesetter and night school student. His degree is in Business Administration. His career led from printing and publishing to contract management. Fascinated by Chinese character fonts, he began translating Chinese poetry almost 20 years ago. He is retired, living in North Carolina with his wife, Mary Lou. He has published five books for Amazon Kindle devices and aps.

Steven Townsend: Mr. Townsend participated in the review of this issue of 21st Century Chinese Poetry. Born in the US but spent considerable time in Europe as a child, Mr.

Townsend writes poetry as well as translates poetry from French, Spanish, and Italian to English. He has published some of his poetic works as Kindle e-books. Mr. Townsend lives in Washington DC.

Poets (listed in alphabetical order):

Niu Qingguo: Mr. Niu was born in 1962 in Gansu Province. Presently he serves as the vice chairman of Gansu Province Writers Association. He is the editor of the capital newspaper of Gansu Province. He has published a collection of poems: *The Ways of My Passion*.

Ren Xianqing: Mr. Ren was born and lives in Shandong Province. He graduated from the Chinese Language Department of Qufu Normal University. He is a member of the Writers' Union of China. He has published two collections of poems: *The Heart with No Boundaries* and *The Heart-Shaped Leaves*.

Sha Ma: Mr. Sha Ma (pen name, born Li Wei) was born in Anhui Province. He began his writing career in early 1980s, and did not focus on poetry until the middle of 1990s. He has won poetry awards in China and has published several collections of poems, including *Poetry by Shama* and *Collection of Poems by Shama*.

Yan Meimei: Ms. Yan was born in Liaoning Province and now lives in Zhejiang Province. She began her writer's career in 2009 (adopting the pen name of Yu Shanyan) and has since published *Collected Poems of Yu Shanyan*. Ms. Yan is a member of the Writers' Union of China. Her poetry can be seen in various poetry journals in China.

Yang Kang: Mr. Yang was born in 1988 in San'xi Province and now studies engineering in Chongqing University. His poetry can be seen in various poetry journals in China. His poem "I Don't like Windy Days" (included in this issue of 21st Century Chinese Poetry) has been very popular among poetry readers and widely circulated on internet.

Yi Hu: Mr. Yi Hu (pen name, born Liu Wen) was born in 1962 in the city of Wuhan by the Yangtze River and still lives there. He has written novels and screenplays for films. His poetry style is imaginative and airy with a unique personal voice.

Wang, Meifu: Ms. Wang is the chief editor and translator of this issue of 21st Century Chinese Poetry. Born and grew up in Taiwan, Meifu Wang earned her BA in Foreign Languages and Literature from National Taiwan University. Her poetry can be seen in various Chinese literary journals. She lives in Washington DC.

Zhang Fanxiu: Mr. Zhang Fanxiu was born 1958 in Hebei Province. He graduated from high school in 1975 and has been a farmer since then. Since 2007 he moved to the remote western region of Liaoning Province and has since produced hundreds of poems that reveal great insight into nature, the land and rural life. His poetry is uniquely rich and lucid in both language and subject matter. His work can be seen in various major literary journals in China. He also has published three collections of poems *Writings from the Moors*, *The Spirit of the Earth*, and *Only the Earth*.

Cover Page Artist:

<Graffiti at 798 Beijing Art Gallery> (Photograph), by Steven Townsend, Washington DC

Contact Information

You are welcome to write to the editors of *21st Century Chinese Poetry* at the following address, and we will try our best to answer your questions.

editor@modernchinesepoetry.com

Made in the USA
Lexington, KY
27 October 2012